Level B · Book 3

QuickReads®
A Research-Based Fluency Program

Elfrieda H. Hiebert, Ph.D.

MODERN CURRICULUM PRESS

Pearson Learning Group

Program Reviewers and Consultants

Dr. Barbara A. Baird
Director of Federal Programs/Richardson ISD
Richardson, TX

Dr. Kate Kinsella
Dept. of Secondary Education and Step to College Program
San Francisco State University
San Francisco, CA

Pat Sears
Early Child Coordinator/Virginia Beach Public Schools
Virginia Beach, VA

Dr. Judith B. Smith
Supervisor of ESOL and World and Classical Languages/Baltimore City Public Schools
Baltimore, MD

The following people have contributed to the development of this product:

Art and Design: Adriano Farinella, Dorothea Fox, Salita Mehta,
  Janice Noto-Helmers, Evelyn O'Shea, Dan Thomas

Editorial: Lynn W. Kloss

Manufacturing: Michele Uhl

Marketing: Connie Buck

Production: Laura Benford-Sullivan, Jeffrey Engel

Publishing Operations: Jennifer Van Der Heide

Modern
Curriculum
Press

Pearson Learning Group

1-800-321-3106
www.pearsonlearning.com

Contents

SOCIAL STUDIES

Children's Games

Games of Then and Now 10

Games with Balls 12

Games with Toys 14

Games of Running and Hopping 16

Games with Words 18

Children's Games Review 20

 Connect Your Ideas 23

Contents

SOCIAL STUDIES

Transportation Then and Now

Transportation in America 24

Trains 26

Bicycles 28

Cars 30

Airplanes 32

Transportation Then and Now Review 34

 Connect Your Ideas 37

SOCIAL STUDIES

Life in Colonial America

What Was Colonial America? 38

An Important New Food 40

Houses 42

School 44

Shadow Stories 46

Life in Colonial America Review 48

 Connect Your Ideas 51

Contents

SCIENCE **Magnets**

What Do Magnets Do? 52

Make Your Own Magnet 54

North and South 56

Finding the Right Direction 58

Everyday Uses of Magnets 60

Magnets Review 62

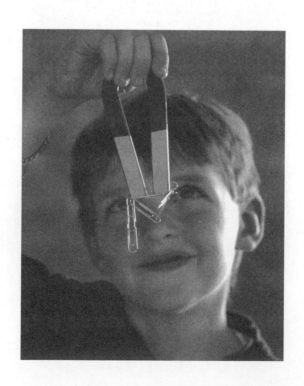 Connect Your Ideas 65

SCIENCE **Forces Around Us**

Push and Pull 66

Work and Play 68

Energy and Work 70

Up and Down 72

Smooth and Rough 74

Forces Around Us Review 76

Connect Your Ideas 79

Contents

SCIENCE **Thinking Like a Scientist**

Asking Questions 80

Using Your Senses 82

Taking Notes 84

Doing Tests 86

A Shark Scientist 88

Thinking Like a Scientist Review 90

 Connect Your Ideas 93

Reading Log 94

Self-Check Graph 96

Acknowledgments

All photographs © Pearson Learning unless otherwise noted

Cover: Richard Cummins/Corbis.

Interior: 3: © B. Bachmann/The Image Works Incorporated. 5: Wood River Gallery/PictureQuest. 6: Phil Schermeister/ Corbis. 7: © Tim Davis/Photo Researchers, Inc. 8: © Doug Martin/ Photo Researchers, Inc. 10: Nancy Shechan/Index Stock Imagery/PictureQuest. 14: Courtesy, Colonial Williamsburg Foundation, photo by Pearson Education. 16: © B. Bachmann/The Image Works Incorporated. 18: Ryan McVay/PhotoDisc, Inc/Getty Images, Inc. 24: Bettmann/Corbis. 26: Getty Images, Inc. 28: The Granger Collection. 32: Bob Battersby/©Eye Ubiquitous/Corbis. 38: Wood River Gallery/PictureQuest. 40: Mitch Hrdlicka/PhotoDisc, Inc./Getty Images, Inc. 42: G. E. Kidder Smith/Corbis. 44: Bettmann/Corbis. 46: PhotoDisc, Inc./ Getty Images, Inc. 52: © Lon C. Diehl/PhotoEdit. 54: Erin Hogan/ PhotoDisc, Inc./Getty Images, Inc. 56: Tony Freeman/PhotoEdit. 58: Phil Schermeister/Corbis. 60: Eastcott-Momatiuk/The Image Works. 66: © Myrleen Ferguson Cate/PhotoEdit. 68: Cassy Cohen/PhotoEdit. 70: Karl Weatherly/PhotoDisc, Inc./Getty Images, Inc. 72: © Tim Davis/Photo Researchers, Inc. 80: © Doug Martin/ Photo Researchers, Inc. 82: Rob Crandall/Stock Connection/ PictureQuest. 84, 86: Michael Newman/PhotoEdit. 88: James L. Stanfield/ © National Geographic Society

Children's Games

Some games children play today are like
games children played long ago.

Games of Then and Now

Today, children play many kinds of games with their friends. They use toys or balls to play some games. They[25] hide and find each other in other games. Long ago, children played with toys and balls, too. They also played games of hide-and-seek.[50]

Long ago, children had different names and rules for some games that children play today. However, most games that children play today are the same[75] games that children played long ago.

Today, children play some games on computers. Even tic-tac-toe, which children now play on computers, was played[100] by children long ago. They just played it on sand or dirt.[112]

Children's Games

Today, rubber balls are used
by children to play games.

Games with Balls

Balls come in many sizes, but most are round. You can play many different games with balls. You can throw and kick[25] a ball. You can hit a ball with a stick. You can run with a ball. You can jump with a ball and throw it[50] through a hoop.

Children have always played games with balls. However, the balls used today are different from the balls that were used in games[75] of long ago. Long ago, balls were made of animal skins, wood, or even clay. Those balls did not bounce. Today, most balls are made[100] of rubber. With rubber balls, children can play games where the ball bounces.[113]

Children's Games

Long ago, children rolled hoops
taken from wooden barrels.

Games with Toys

Over the years, children have played with toys like blocks, dolls, and stuffed animals. Today, children play with the same kinds of[25] toys. However, today's toys look a little different from the toys of long ago.

Long ago, most toys were made at home. Dolls might be[50] made of old socks. Round hoops for rolling on the ground might be taken from old wooden barrels.

Today, children's toys usually come from stores.[75] Many toys are made of plastic, not old socks or barrels. Plastic can be used to make almost any toy. Many toys use batteries. With[100] batteries, toy trucks can move by themselves. With batteries, dolls can talk.[112]

Children's Games

Hopscotch is a game that has been played by children for many years.

Games of Running and Hopping

For hundreds of years, children have played games in which they run and hop. In tag, the person who is[25] "it" runs after people and tries to tag them. In many games, people run with a ball. Sometimes people just run to see who is[50] the fastest runner.

In hopscotch, children take turns hopping through ten squares. On every turn, a player throws a stone called a marker into one[75] of the squares. To stay in a game of hopscotch, players have to throw their marker in the right square and hop over squares with[100] markers. Running and hopping games have been played in many ways for many years.[114]

Children's Games

Children often play word games by saying
words and clapping their hands.

Games with Words

Word games can be played anywhere. Word games do not need any toys or balls. To play a word game, all you[25] need are some friends and words.

Some word games like "I Spy" are guessing games. In "I Spy," one person picks something in the room,[50] like a red lamp. The person then gives the other players a clue by saying, "I spy with my little eye something that is red."[75] The other players take turns guessing what the person sees.

In another word game, children clap as they say the words. The clapping games use[100] poems. Games like these have been played by children for many years, too.[113]

Children's Games

Write words that will help you remember what you learned.

Games of Then and Now

_____

_____

_____

_____

Games with Balls

_____

_____

_____

_____

Games with Toys

_____

_____

_____

_____

Games of Running and Hopping

_____

_____

_____

_____

Games with Words

_____

_____

_____

_____

Games of Then and Now

1. Another good name for "Games of Then and Now" is ____

Ⓐ "Long-Ago Games."

Ⓑ "The Games Children Play."

Ⓒ "Games of Today."

Ⓓ "Rules for Games."

2. How are games of today different from games children played long ago?

_____

_____

_____

Games with Balls

1. "Games with Balls" is MAINLY about ____

Ⓐ balls that can be hit with a stick.

Ⓑ games that do not use balls.

Ⓒ different balls and games to play with a ball.

Ⓓ how to make balls for games.

2. How are balls today different from balls of long ago?

_____

_____

_____

Games with Toys

1. How are toys today different from toys of long ago?

Ⓐ Toys today may come from stores and be made of plastic.

Ⓑ Toys today are made of wooden barrels and old socks.

Ⓒ Toys today are made only for young children.

Ⓓ Toys today are dolls and stuffed animals.

2. Retell two facts you learned in "Games with Toys."

_____

_____

_____

Games of Running and Hopping

1. The main idea of "Games of Running and Hopping" is _____

Ⓐ how to make a new running and hopping game.

Ⓑ why children like running and hopping games.

Ⓒ that running and hopping games have been played for many years.

Ⓓ why people play tag and hopscotch differently today.

2. List three running and hopping games.

_____

_____

_____

Games with Words

1. What are two kinds of word games?

   Ⓐ running games and clapping games
   Ⓑ color games and guessing games
   Ⓒ guessing games and clapping games
   Ⓓ clapping games and ball games

2. What do people need to play word games?

   _____

   _____

   _____

Connect Your Ideas

1. How are the things used in games long ago different from the things used in games today?

   _____

   _____

   _____

2. Would you rather play the games of long ago or the games of today? Why?

   _____

   _____

   _____

Transportation Then and Now

Before cars were invented, people rode in coaches that were pulled by horses.

Airplanes

1. Another good name for "Airplanes" is _____
   - (A) "Airplanes Then and Now."
   - (B) "Fast Airplanes."
   - (C) "Transportation Today."
   - (D) "How Airplanes Work."

2. How has air travel changed from the first airplanes?

Air travel has changed from the first airplane in these ways; ~~They~~ have become faster and they can hold more people.

Connect Your Ideas

1. How do people travel differently today from 100 years ago?

2. What kind of transportation do you think people might use 100 years from now?

Life in Colonial America

Ships like this one brought people
from England to North America.

What Was Colonial America?

Almost 400 years ago, a ship brought people from England to live in North America. After that, many more ships brought[25] people from England and many other places. The people lived in 13 places in North America that were called colonies.

The colonies were far from[50] England, but people in England ruled the colonies. In the year 1776, the people in the 13 colonies told England that they had made their[75] own country. They called this country the United States. When we talk about colonial America, we talk about the 13 colonies before 1776. Life in[100] colonial America was different from life in the United States today.[111]

Life in Colonial America

Corn was an important food in colonial America.

An Important New Food

When the first ships of colonists reached North America, the colonists had very little food left. The Native Americans shared food[25] with them. The Native Americans had food that was new to the colonists. Corn was the most important of the new foods. It was not[50] hard to grow corn in North America.

Corn had many uses. Corn on the cob was good to eat. Dried corn could be ground into[75] flour. The flour was used for baking. One kind of dried corn could be made into popcorn. Corn was used for animal food, too. In[100] winter, animals were fed the long stems of the corn plant.[111]

Life in Colonial America

The colonists built houses with steep roofs
so the snow could slide off the roofs.

Houses

As soon as they landed in North America, people had to build homes. Their first homes were made out of logs that they cut[25] into pieces. There were often big cracks between the logs. The cracks were filled with mud and grass. If the mud and grass fell out,[50] rain and snow came into the house.

Later, the colonists built houses that looked like their old homes in England. Many houses had flat roofs.[75] Soon, the colonists found that they needed to change their houses. It snowed more in parts of the 13 colonies than in England. People began[100] to build houses with steep roofs. Steep roofs let the snow slide off the roofs.[115]

Life in Colonial America

Boys and girls went to Dame Schools.

School

In colonial America, children first went to Dame Schools. Dame Schools were in teachers' houses. Teachers used hornbooks to teach reading in Dame Schools.[25] A hornbook was a block of wood with a page of letters or words on it. It was called a hornbook because a thin sheet[50] of cow's horn was put over the letters and words. The sheet of cow's horn kept the letters and words clean. A clean hornbook could[75] be used for many years.

When girls could read, they stopped going to school. Boys went to another school where boys of all ages were[100] in one class. They had to sit still. They could not move around or talk.[115]

Life in Colonial America

When they told stories by the fireplace,
people sometimes made shadows of animals.

Shadow Stories

Even children worked hard in colonial America. Yet, there were times for fun, too. Children played tag. They skated on ice. During the[25] long, cold winters, children played games inside. While children played games close to the warm fireplace, someone told a story. Sometimes, storytellers would put their[50] hands in front of the fire. The firelight made a shadow on the wall. Storytellers would shape their hands to make the shadows look like[75] animals or people from the story.

You can tell shadow stories, too. Ask someone to point a flashlight at a wall. Hold your hands away[100] from the flashlight. Now make your hands into the shapes of different animals.[113]

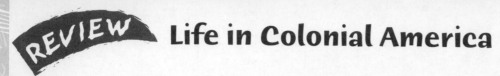

REVIEW Life in Colonial America

Write words that will help you remember what you learned.

What Was Colonial America?

_____

_____

_____

_____

An Important New Food

_____

_____

_____

_____

Houses

_____

_____

_____

_____

School

_____

_____

_____

_____

Shadow Stories

_____

_____

_____

_____

What Was Colonial America?

1. How did people begin the North American colonies?

   Ⓐ People began to live in towns in England.

   Ⓑ People moved from England to North America.

   Ⓒ People moved from the United States to England.

   Ⓓ People moved from the United States to the colonies.

2. What was colonial America?

   _____

   _____

   _____

An Important New Food

1. Another good name for "An Important New Food" is _____

   Ⓐ "Sharing Food."

   Ⓑ "A New Food for the Colonists."

   Ⓒ "Food from England."

   Ⓓ "Native American Foods."

2. Name three ways the colonists used corn.

   _____

   _____

   _____

REVIEW **Life in Colonial America**

Houses

1. What is the main idea of "Houses"?

Ⓐ how colonists learned to build houses from mud

Ⓑ how houses have changed over the years

Ⓒ what houses in colonial America were like

Ⓓ how to build a house in North America today

2. What three different kinds of houses did the colonists build?

_____

_____

_____

School

1. "School" is MAINLY about _____

Ⓐ girls going to school in colonial America.

Ⓑ how children went to school in colonial America.

Ⓒ the books students read in colonial America.

Ⓓ what teachers were like in colonial America.

2. What was school like in colonial America?

_____

_____

_____

Shadow Stories

1. What is a shadow story?

   Ⓐ a story about shadows

   Ⓑ a story about games that is told at night

   Ⓒ a story that is acted out

   Ⓓ a story told by making shadows on a wall

2. Name two ways children had fun in colonial America.

   _____

   _____

   _____

Connect Your Ideas

1. Name three ways that life changed for the colonists who came to live in North America.

   _____

   _____

   _____

2. What would your life have been like in colonial America?

   _____

   _____

   _____

Magnets

Magnets can hold papers on refrigerator doors.

What Do Magnets Do?

Many people have pictures on the door of their refrigerator. If you look closely, you will see that the pictures are[25] held in place by magnets. Most magnets are made of iron. They stick to other things with iron in them. Magnets stick to refrigerator doors[50] because refrigerator doors have iron in them.

The magnetic force holding the magnet to the door acts right through the picture. If you tried to[75] hang a picture on a wall using a magnet, the magnet and the picture would just fall to the floor. Why don't they stay up?[100] They don't stay up because most walls do not have iron in them.[113]

Magnets

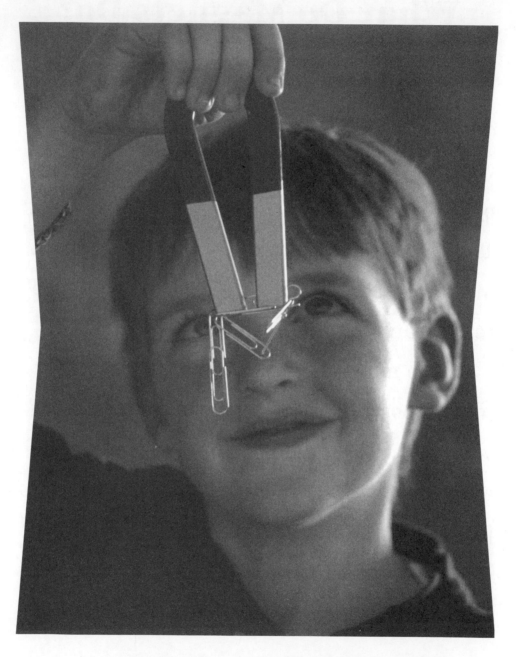

Magnets can pick up paper clips because
paper clips have iron in them.

Make Your Own Magnet

You can make your own magnet with a pin. Pins can be magnets because pins have iron in them. Pennies cannot[25] be magnets because pennies do not have iron in them.

To make a magnet, drag a pin along one end of a magnet. Drag the[50] pin only in one direction. Don't move it back and forth. Drag the pin in the same direction about 25 times. Your pin should now[75] act like a magnet. You will not be able to pick up heavy things with your new magnet, but you should be able to pick[100] up light things. See if your pin will pick up a paper clip.[113]

The poles of these magnets are pulling them together.

North and South

The ends of magnets are called "poles." One end of a magnet is its north pole. The other end is its south[25] pole. The poles of magnets, not the magnet's center, pull things to them. When there is more than one magnet, it matters what direction the[50] magnets are to each other.

If you put two magnets together, the magnets stick together or push each other away. When the north poles or[75] the south poles of two magnets face each other, the magnets push each other away. However, if you put the north pole of one magnet[100] against the south pole of another magnet, they will stick together.[111]

Magnets

The magnetic needle on a compass
helps people find the right direction.

Finding the Right Direction

It can be fun to get magnets to stick to each other. However, magnets can help people, too. The Earth has[25] a lot of iron inside it. This iron and some other forces help Earth act like a really big magnet.

A magnetic needle will point[50] to the magnetic north pole of Earth. This is how a compass works. No matter which way a compass is turned, its needle points to[75] the magnetic north pole of Earth. With a compass, people can always tell which way is north. With a compass, people can go to new[100] places and not get lost. They can always find the right direction.[112]

Magnets

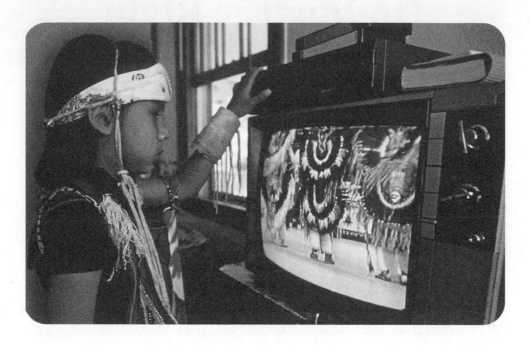

Magnets make the pictures on videotapes.

Everyday Uses of Magnets

Magnets are used in many ways. Some ways are to hold pictures on refrigerators and to find directions with compasses. The[25] bankcards that people use to buy things in stores have magnets. The black strips on the back of bankcards are tiny magnets. These magnets store[50] information that tells the bank about the person.

Videotapes also use magnets. Like bankcards, videotapes have tiny magnets. The VCR uses them to make the[75] picture. The magnets that are in bankcards and videotapes are so tiny that you can't see them. However, these magnets act just like a magnet[100] you might make from a pin or the magnets on a refrigerator.[112]

Write words that will help you remember what you learned.

What Do Magnets Do?

_____

_____

_____

_____

Make Your Own Magnet

_____

_____

_____

_____

North and South

_____

_____

_____

_____

Finding the Right Direction

_____

_____

_____

_____

Everyday Uses of Magnets

_____

_____

_____

_____

What Do Magnets Do?

1. "What Do Magnets Do?" is MAINLY about _____

    Ⓐ how magnets work.

    Ⓑ different kinds of magnets.

    Ⓒ the many uses of magnets.

    Ⓓ magnets on refrigerator doors.

2. What do magnets do?

_____

_____

_____

Make Your Own Magnet

1. What is the main idea of "Make Your Own Magnet"?

    Ⓐ how pins are magnets

    Ⓑ how to use a magnet

    Ⓒ how to make a magnet

    Ⓓ why people make magnets

2. How can you make a pin into a magnet?

_____

_____

_____

North and South

1. What are poles on magnets?

Ⓐ the parts of magnets that are hot

Ⓑ the parts of magnets that go the same way

Ⓒ the ends of magnets

Ⓓ the centers of magnets

2. How can you make two magnets stick together?

_____

_____

_____

Finding the Right Direction

1. How can magnets help people?

Ⓐ Magnets can help people find Earth.

Ⓑ Magnets are giant compasses.

Ⓒ Magnets can keep people from getting lost.

Ⓓ Magnetic needles have iron inside them.

2. What does a compass do?

_____

_____

_____

Everyday Uses of Magnets

1. Another good name for "Everyday Uses of Magnets" is _____

   Ⓐ "Magnets in Your Home."

   Ⓑ "Magnets People Wear."

   Ⓒ "Magnets in School."

   Ⓓ "The Many Uses of Magnets."

2. What are three ways we use magnets?

_____

_____

_____

Connect Your Ideas

1. Name three things that a magnet can stick to.

_____

_____

_____

2. What do you think is the most important way to use magnets? Why?

_____

_____

_____

Forces Around Us

You can move a wagon
by pushing it or pulling it.

Push and Pull

You and your friends are playing with a wagon. One friend gets into the wagon and asks you to move it. How[25] can you move the wagon? You can push it or pull it. When you push or pull the wagon, you use force. By using force,[50] you can move the wagon from place to place.

What if your friend asks you to make the wagon move faster? You can use more[75] force. If your friend is small, it will not take much force to go faster. However, if your friend is big, it will take a[100] lot more force to go faster. Force makes things move.[110]

Forces Around Us

You use force when you move a toy car.

Work and Play

You are playing with a toy car. Whenever you move the toy car, we say that you are doing work. Work happens[25] when a force is used to move something.

If you use a lot of force to move something, you are doing a lot of work.[50] It is more work to move a box of toy cars than to move one toy car. Even when you play, you may be doing[75] work.

If you push a real car but it does not move, you are not doing work. Why? The force you use is too small[100] to move the car. A force has to move something to do work.[113]

Forces Around Us

You are doing work when
you are riding your bicycle.

Energy and Work

When you take out the trash, you do work. When you lift a heavy book, you do work. When you and your[25] friends ride your bikes, you all do work. Work happens when you use force to make something move. Yet, how does the force do the[50] work? The force does the work by using energy.

You must have energy to do work. If you do a lot of work, you use[75] a lot of energy. If you do just a little work, you don't use very much energy. You get energy from food. Cars get energy[100] from gas. If there is energy, work can be done.[110]

Forces Around Us

Gravity keeps you from jumping up too high.

Up and Down

Why can't you jump ten feet in the air? Gravity holds you down. Gravity is the force that pulls you back to[25] Earth.

Why can you toss a ball ten feet in the air? It does not take much force to toss a ball because a ball[50] does not have much mass. It takes less force to move things with less mass.

You have more mass than a ball. So it would[75] take more force for you to jump ten feet in the air than to toss a ball ten feet in the air. Moving an object[100] with a lot of mass against the force of gravity takes a lot of energy.[115]

Forces Around Us

Friction makes it hard to drag a chair over a rug.

Smooth and Rough

If you have ever tried to move an object like a heavy chair, you know about friction. A heavy chair is hard[25] to drag over something rough like a rug. The chair does not move easily because it rubs against the rug. The force that makes it[50] hard to drag one thing over another is called friction.

A heavy chair is easy to move over a slick floor. That is because there[75] is less friction between objects and smooth surfaces, such as a slick floor. There is more friction between objects and rough surfaces, such as a[100] rug. If there is less friction, it is easier to move something.[112]

Forces Around Us

Write words that will help you remember what you learned.

Push and Pull

_____

_____

_____

_____

Work and Play

_____

_____

_____

_____

Energy and Work

_____

_____

_____

_____

Up and Down

_____

_____

_____

_____

Smooth and Rough

_____

_____

_____

_____

Push and Pull

1. What can happen when you use force?

Ⓐ You can make a wagon.

Ⓑ You can make something move.

Ⓒ You can play a game with your friends.

Ⓓ You can go from place to place.

2. Retell two facts you learned in "Push and Pull."

_____

_____

_____

Work and Play

1. Another good name for "Work and Play" is ____

Ⓐ "Force and Work."

Ⓑ "Playing with Cars."

Ⓒ "How to Work."

Ⓓ "Moving Things."

2. When does work happen?

_____

_____

_____

Forces Around Us

Energy and Work

1. Why do you need energy?

Ⓐ to sit still

Ⓑ to get force

Ⓒ to make more energy

Ⓓ to do work

2. How do people and cars get energy?

_____

_____

_____

Up and Down

1. What is "Up and Down" MAINLY about?

Ⓐ what mass is

Ⓑ what different forces are

Ⓒ how gravity works

Ⓓ why people can jump ten feet in the air

2. What is gravity?

_____

_____

_____

Smooth and Rough

1. Friction is the force that _____

    Ⓐ makes it hard to drag one thing over another.

    Ⓑ keeps you from jumping high in the air.

    Ⓒ tells you when something is smooth or rough.

    Ⓓ gives you energy to move things.

2. Why is it easier to move something over a smooth surface than over a rough surface?

    _____

    _____

    _____

Connect Your Ideas

1. Tell about two forces you learned about.

    _____

    _____

    _____

2. Name two ways you use energy every day.

    _____

    _____

    _____

Thinking Like a Scientist

Scientists use their senses to
get information about the world.

Asking Questions

The word *science* means "knowledge" or "information." Scientists are people who study the world to get knowledge or information. Scientists ask how things[25] work. They use their senses to get knowledge. They think about what they learn. First, scientists ask questions. Then, they look for answers to questions.[50]

Where do the colors of a rainbow come from? There are many colors in a rainbow: red, orange, yellow, green, blue, and purple. Light doesn't[75] look like it has color. Yet, rainbows have the colors red, orange, yellow, green, blue, and purple. What happens to the colors when the rainbow[100] goes away? When you ask questions like these, you are thinking like a scientist.[114]

Thinking Like a Scientist

Your senses can help you learn
about the world around you.

Using Your Senses

To get new knowledge, you use parts of your body called your senses. Your senses help you see, hear, touch, taste, and[25] smell. You see with your eyes. Your ears let you hear sounds. You touch things with your skin, usually your hands. You taste with your[50] mouth. You use your nose to find out how things smell.

Scientists use their senses to get new information, too. However, scientists are careful in[75] how they use their senses. They never taste unknown things. Scientists are careful about what they touch. Scientists also take care of their eyes, ears,[100] and noses when they work with things that can hurt them.[111]

Thinking Like a Scientist

These young scientists take notes
as they study the world.

Taking Notes

Scientists study the world to get information. Then, scientists take notes about what they learn. They take notes with pictures and numbers, not[25] just words. Scientists who study the colors in sunlight might write about the colors they see. They also might write about the colors they don't[50] see.

Scientists use their notes to see what is the same and what is different about things. Scientists have found that the colors in a[75] rainbow can be seen through a three-sided piece of glass called a prism. When sunlight passes through a prism, the sunlight comes out as[100] bands of color. Scientists use their notes about color to learn more about sunlight.[114]

Thinking Like a Scientist

Tests help scientists see if their guesses are right.

Doing Tests

Scientists use their notes to make guesses about how things work. Scientists do tests to see if their guesses are right. Scientists now[25] know that the colors of the rainbow are in sunlight all the time. However, something like a prism is needed to bring the colors out.[50] You can do tests like a scientist, too. Just use your senses and take notes about what you learn.

You can test the colors in[75] sunlight. Poke a small hole in a piece of tinfoil. Place the tinfoil over the lens of a flashlight. Now take a CD into a[100] dark room. Shine the flashlight onto the CD. What do you see?[112]

Thinking Like a Scientist

Eugenie Clark studies sharks by
asking questions about them.

A Shark Scientist

Eugenie Clark is a scientist who studies sharks. Eugenie began asking questions like a scientist when she was nine years old. That's[25] when she got a fish tank as a gift. She made notes and pictures about the fish.

Many people think that danger comes from big[50] sharks. However, Eugenie Clark thinks that sharks may face more danger from people than people do from sharks. She found that the biggest shark of[75] all, the whale shark, eats only small sea animals and plants. Eugenie Clark learned about sharks by using her senses, taking notes, and doing tests[100] on sharks. That information will help people understand how to safely live with sharks.[114]

Thinking Like a Scientist

Write words that will help you remember what you learned.

Asking Questions

_____

_____

_____

_____

Using Your Senses

_____

_____

_____

_____

Taking Notes

_____

_____

_____

_____

Doing Tests

_____

_____

_____

_____

A Shark Scientist

_____

_____

_____

_____

Asking Questions

1. A scientist is someone who _____

   Ⓐ uses force to do work.

   Ⓑ writes stories about the world.

   Ⓒ studies the world to get knowledge.

   Ⓓ studies things that happened long ago.

2. How can you think like a scientist?

_____

_____

_____

Using Your Senses

1. What are your senses?

   Ⓐ the way you use your nose to learn how things smell

   Ⓑ touching, seeing, hearing, thinking, and jumping

   Ⓒ how you learn about other people

   Ⓓ sceing, hearing, touching, tasting, and smelling

2. How are scientists careful with their senses?

_____

_____

_____

Thinking Like a Scientist

Taking Notes

1. "Taking Notes" is MAINLY about ____

Ⓐ how scientists take and use notes.

Ⓑ how scientists draw pictures.

Ⓒ where scientists get ideas.

Ⓓ how scientists know what to study.

2. What do scientists do with their notes?

_____

_____

_____

Doing Tests

1. Another good name for "Doing Tests" is ____

Ⓐ "Scientists Use Their Senses."

Ⓑ "Guesses and Tests."

Ⓒ "The Colors of the Rainbow."

Ⓓ "Taking Good Notes."

2. Why do scientists do tests?

_____

_____

_____

A Shark Scientist

1. The main idea of "A Shark Scientist" is _____

   (A) Eugenie Clark's work as a shark scientist.

   (B) how shark scientists work.

   (C) the kinds of sharks Eugenie Clark studies.

   (D) why sharks face danger from people.

2. What did Eugenie Clark learn about sharks?

   _____

   _____

   _____

Connect Your Ideas

1. How can you think like a scientist every day?

   _____

   _____

   _____

2. What would you like to study if you were a scientist?

   _____

   _____

   _____

Reading Log • Level B • Book 3

	I Read This	New Words I Learned	New Facts I Learned	What Else I Want to Learn About This Subject
Children's Games				
Games of Then and Now				
Games with Balls				
Games with Toys				
Games of Running and Hopping				
Games with Words				
Transportation Then and Now				
Transportation in America				
Trains				
Bicycles				
Cars				
Airplanes				
Life in Colonial America				
What Was Colonial America?				
An Important New Food				
Houses				
School				
Shadow Stories				

	I Read This	New Words I Learned	New Facts I Learned	What Else I Want to Learn About This Subject
Magnets				
What Do Magnets Do?				
Make Your Own Magnet				
North and South				
Finding the Right Direction				
Everyday Uses of Magnets				
Forces Around Us				
Push and Pull				
Work and Play				
Energy and Work				
Up and Down				
Smooth and Rough				
Thinking Like a Scientist				
Asking Questions				
Using Your Senses				
Taking Notes				
Doing Tests				
A Shark Scientist				

Self-Check Graph

Mark your reading rate here.

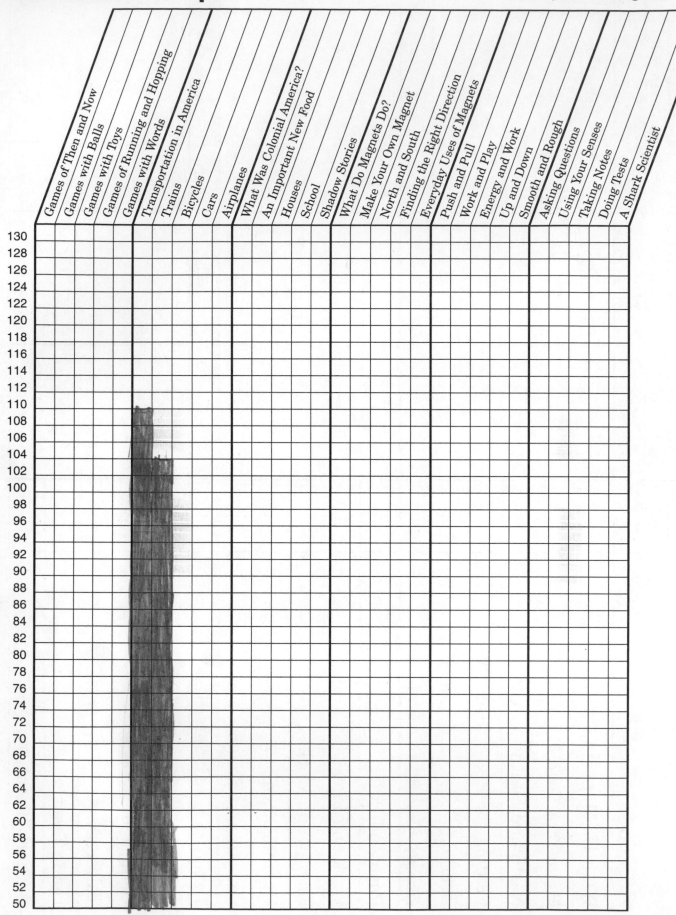

96